UNTO DOGS

poems

STEPHANIE GINESE

Published by Grieveland

Cover Artwork by Carolina Mercado
Cover & Book Design by Angelo Maneage

ISBN 978-1-7353527-6-3

GRVLND | www.grieveland.com

an italian & a puerto rican walk into a bar & give birth to this atrocity

My father's name finds me dizzy in the ocean
Crying splints of glass   A mangled compass lodged in my throat

This is so 1492 of me

My father's name brings me where everything is new
But I am an Amerik³an daughter that knows nothing
of   land
or   opportunity

& so
I am claiming my father's name for mine

Treaty of Territory **[SELF / LITTLE BODY / I]**

I, hereby, am a fleet of disease upon	my father's name
twining chains around the ankles of	my father's name
testing the sharpness of my blade on	my father's name
riding on the back of	my father's name
cutting the hands off	my father's name
ravaging the manhood of	my father's name
feeding to my dogs the supple babes of	my father's name
ending the empire of	my father's name
birthing a new nation with	my father's name

I've tried to find the meaning of my father's name & come up empty

Therefore, I give my own meaning to my father's name

Hereby, this atrocious history is now my father's name

07/23/2022

6

"Once I was a shedder of blood & the great eagle took me in his claws & came into my mouth & ate thereof. He traded me for figs & oil & wine. He drank of me & caused me shame. "

FROM THE PLAY '45 MERCY STREET' BY ANNE SEXTON

"The womb is something that I'd throw into the garbage if I could."

IRENE VILAR

[a welcoming from the angel of tourism]

there is a small ounce of blackspace on the mole that rests above the god of my understanding's lip. where the dead & the unborn gather once the stars have settled. mythic beasts of detriment & dare tonguing the lucid river that cuts through this land of origin. call it Eden, call it Hell. depending on whom you ask. the place one goes when the last of the fight crawls from their mouths. Look closer at some of the wild things that roam under this hibiscus sky. open wholly, so you can bear witness to the story of a new god. a triple mooned god. watch as She creates entire galaxies with a pinch of sugar & the emptiness of a promise.

you can do this too, you know. be an alchemist, a saint, a good daughter. turn choice into a reckoning. history into splayed hip bones carving up the darkest parts.

if you are ready to know salvation at the cost of a most merciless truth

                   because   everything has a price

                                    my dear.

        then come &

sever Little Body   from Self.

leave Little Body   dancing by the river

& Self running   towards the   last   atomic   moon.

☽

GLADYS, (candied waxing crescent) daughter of THE Lolita Lebrón, has the top three buttons undone on her blouse. Bastard babygirl of a cane sugar daddy. Is on her way to school, sucking on bitter fruit. Limonada spit running down her chin on the heaviest day of storm season. She is a small wonder, contemplating the loom of a wedding instead of a quinceañera. She realizes she will be a bride before she is a woman & halts a nauseous moment. Admires the confectious sky. Flashes a mouthful of skeletons at someone who isn't there. Pulling herself up to sit atop an earnest wall, feet dangling over the edge. Her legs, a howl apart.

IRENE, (fullest of redemptive moons) granddaughter of THE Lolita Lebrón, is playing mother. Again. Or better yet, playing with the idea of mothering. It is her favorite dress to put on. Sometimes, she wears a hospital gown when she has spent too much time seducing Death. After all, she is her mother's daughter & this is a story of the masters we inherit. A compulsive deity, holding handfuls of lace as black as the space her mother, Gladys, left behind as she poured her body out of the speeding car. Fifteen satellites as steady as unborn cries orbit the lumen of Irene. One day, all of this will be memories trapped in the pages of a mirror. Now, it is the heaviest of what she carries.

☾

THE LOLITA LEBRÓN, (atomic waning crescent) is storming the gates of Heaven. Left fist raised high. The terrifying red of her cinnamon gum lips parting to machinegun spit the words I did not come here to kill. I came here to die. St. Peter throws the gate keys into the celestial winds & runs for the meringue hills. Lolita enters; an epic story no one who comes after can escape. The angels crown her Heaven's most beautiful. Lolita! Lolita! The choir begins. She takes the gilded halo into her mouth. Gnashes it between her ready teeth. An unloaded clip, her most celebrated gospel.

la hija [the good daughter's prayer]

the mothers who came before me refused soft hands over continuing the fight

never tolerated being under someone's rule

they knew life was as perishable as plantains the moment before they become

                                                        maduros

the mothers who came before me were all

                                        machete tongued

                                        rum drunk

                                        cracked chicken neck

                                        a little piqué in the coffee

they are all g o n e   yet still breathing within the wildest parts of me

                    I am made in their

                        Vision

la operación aka **when he asks if I'm on birth control**

Between the 1930s & the 1970s, one-third of the female population of Puerto Rico
was sterilized, making this the highest rate of sterilization in the world.

- Center for Latin Studies, University of Pittsburgh

Fertility: a gift

   or a curse

                 dependent on skin color

        or   where one watches the stars   from

    /

the women of Puerto Rico are considered

                  more   animal

                  than   human

           mothering machines tucked into mountains

[ENTER **AMERIK³A**] : a Dr. Frankenstein with less fervor

                              & more genocidal tendencies

               tying tubes into nots

                             or noteveragains

a life sentence sentenced

          but here lies no more life

               so what is there to give ?

see

the curse be that the women of Puerto Rico hold so much passion in the plexus

Christh   himself   becomes a chorus of shudders each time our knees   part

such a deep devotion to miracles   we cannot stop imitating them

like hands   passing across the skin of the conga

                    honoring the ritual of Creation so fully

those imperialist parasites   pass   law(s)

                    govern   body(s)

to try & quiet   the showy nature

                    of God

                    Herself

& I once read an article about a biologist at Berkeley who said Puerto Rican women were the closest example of the perfect human that exists due to the mix of blood/sugar/salt & maybe that's why Amerik³a wanted to stop the breeding of a people it didn't regard as perfect or even as people but more so a by product that overproduces &

I know this is not the answer to the question

but

hijadelagranputa

Hija de la Gran Puta   [translation]   *Daughter of the Greatest Bitch*

this is the term of endearment passed down from my mother & her mother

offered up like a herringbone like it was sworn in the pages of a familial holy book

when I was a little puta I mean girl I mean too young to know the difference

I thought it all one long word   a necronomicon of sorts that would conjure a bitch queen mother

from the potholes on our street   a wild haired temptress with patent heeled paws

a lipstick shade as dark as the fourth days blood & a mole painted right above Her dark waiting m

what I've always wanted to know is

who is this Great Bitch   *Most High Bitch*   *God Bitch*

what of myself would I see echoed in the negative of Her eyes

& if She were to meet Death unwelcomed   like all the bitches that I love do

will I then be called to ascend the throne

be cast unto the darkest side of the moon only to return

when bitches of a particular kind of wicked summon me

or if I am someday called to sit at the paws of Mami Puta

will She lovingly encourage my insolent nature

mother me the way mortal mothers never could?

what I do know is if there were ever a legacy to live towards

this   I would consider   the most fitting

confession

FADE IN:

EMPTY ROOM - SINGLE SPOTLIGHT
(Self)

SELF SITS ON THE FLOOR, HALOED BY THE SPOTLIGHT & A PLUME OF SMOKE.

> SELF
>
> I will offer this body to a howling god. Pray it weighs enough sacrifice to salvage the most infernal parts.
>
> But I will not repent for these sins. For desiring a good story more than I do my own peace.

SELF TAKES ANOTHER HIT.   EXHALES.

> SELF
>
> The thing is, I am always willing to dance for my food. See these soles? A scabbed stigmata of misfortune.
>
> & what of my love? A filterless cigarette. A burning drag. Most times, the funniest girl at the party. Until sunlight trespasses the dust spangled sill &
>
>   the laugh track untangles from her teeth.

de·col·o·nize

verb

/ I decolonize my damp map underwear / shove them into a mouth "aww"-ing the **O** in de ˙c**O** / I'm so decolonized I take my love pill-less & raw / de-colon : to remove the ass of / this country / so pain in my ass / I pledge decolonization to the colony of my colostomy / colostomy : an opening so formed / the colony is a port / Little Body is a port / we are both openings so formed / colon: a portion or limb / Puerto Rico: world's oldest colony / a choked limb denied blood / supply / this shade of decolonization doesn't go well with my used portions / I'm so coveted that I had to be colonized / God knows / one cannot be / fertile & free

hey God, if enough people misuse the word *decolonize*, does it even make a [sound]?

use over time for: decolonize

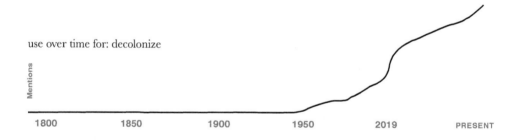

Mentions

| 1800 | 1850 | 1900 | 1950 | 2019 | PRESENT |

1 in **3** women of child bearing age [sterilized]

on sterilization

unoccupied   but that wasn't always the case   case & point there are the children

see, I can make some thing out of no thing
          make a whole country within another country

to sterilize is to make some thing: *free from contamination / disinfected / purified*

I pledge allegiance to Gladys & the 30%
who chose or did not
what is choice   when freedom is a foreign language
silence becomes a body of unfamiliar characters

& the body   who could forget what a pain it is
to constantly have to save what carries your best looking shame

I am gnawing at my hands for the last night in a row
because my palms are two small boats & I am
not well versed in navigating a starless night

however   I am finding
          there is a ripe pleasure in being lost with the only thing that truly belongs to you

& best believe I am leaving with all that I came

Lolita's ghost, Gladys' ghost, & I wrote this poem

before   It   became conquered land
          Borikén
          Land of the Great Lords
          My womb

It   was a holy wilderness
Boriken
Land of the Great Lords
My womb

natural wonder of edenic chaos

                    I am trying to come to terms with my own myth
                                        my own mouth

all the body's   a blued flower
                    a night song
                    an atomic moon

& the sky   a prison on fire
                    a law
                    a history

with   stars   astrewn
            bullets dislodged from the throat of a god

which god? queries a voice from somewhere vast & unending

          the one I created.
          the one I became.

Paca, 1991

you could never be proper name

    could never be

the blood   bloomed   the baby was gone

took you with it   the baby

o negative cannot mix with any other

                    type   of blood   so

body becomes a sour host   foreign object

                  see also: the damn baby

you   Paca   not a home

I   Nuna   not a home   until…

same blood but not but

we could say sisters

same blood   type

we are a type of sisters

                        Paca

I remember the day I said your name

your namename

&youcried&cried&

accused me of growing up

I would've stayed small if that meant you could've

stayed   growing up is the only shame there is

keeping

the women in my family are good at keeping secrets

heirlooms locked away in the buried place

cobwebbed & worm gutted

the dark is   safe

                a

swallowed keys ~~rust~~ rest heavy in belly

g   estating into cryptic fruit

we pretend not to notice

the stench

because what remains mystery

cannot cause harm

& each of us whisper into the hollow space of once children - *we did it*

for the good of

out of love for

to protect

Our selves.

that time I made a joke about all the girls in our history class being part of the plan b team

Julissa & Carmen skip class. Slide into Carmen's car. Pass between them a gallon of iced tea & puff menthol cigarettes. What they will remember most about high school is this blend of sweet & cool freedom haunting their wild mouths. They drive to the Planned Parenthood by the mall.

Alyssa, Jacqi, & I skip class. Pack into Alyssa's car. Swig bottles of pineapple soda & share a freshly freaked Mild. What we will remember most about high school is all of the times that we walked out of it. Our loud mouths announcing our exit. We drive to the Planned Parenthood by the mall.

Stepping into the waiting room, it looks exactly like the history class we are all missing. A collection of good daughters who cannot stop offering their territories to any colonizer with a newly graveled voice & babylong lashes. If all the daughters are here, then the colonizers must be the only ones back in class. Comparing conquests over the restless discourse of ghosts. What they will remember most about high school is all of the girls with the wild & loud, but best of all pretty mouths. What they won't remember is all of the times those mouths cursed their careless names.

undertow

There are lies we hold under our tongues

Weighted coins metal slick with the unsaid

How much history does it take to choke on the present?

I can't help but glare at the shiniest thing in the room when my mind is racing

Start with my voice

Since that is what I am most of all

Faithful only to its sound

However I feel closest to God when hands snake

Charm my throat into a primal   [s i l e n c e]

& that's not as curious a thing as once thought

Fish three pearling moons from my mouth

Notice their brilliance - a luster so dense

It poses the question of choking again & I am transfixed

Three mirrors to reflect an unfavorable truth back at me

Is this how we liberate the stars?

(

seed mapping

Amerik³a offers me a ride home from the party. I am too drunk to accept, but also too drunk not to. I blink myself unconscious in the front seat of Amerik³a's car. I am revived by the thrust of Amerik³a exploiting my conceding limbs. I shoot cannons of stuttered no's into Amerik³a's greedy ear. I am not sure I am here anymore. Amerik³a sends me away filled with what's to come. Afterwards, I cry in the key of *The Star Spangled Banner* & the water cannot get hot enough.

Weeks turn into clean underwear. I tell this to Amerik³a. However, Amerik³a does not believe in facts & I am not surprised. This is what empires do: maraud an exquisite land, deny their mishandling, reduce it to a burial ground. I will come to know the feeling of my feet cradled by stirrups before I know the feeling of those same feet on the gas pedal of a car. Freedom is just a two ton illusion we are convinced is worth dying for. I wish I could be rid of Amerik³a as easily as I am able to be rid of its genetically modified seed.

After my Amerik³an abortion, I will sleep for two days. My dreams are a firework of red rivers & white sheets & blue walls.

birth control pills given during the trials [**3x** the current strength]

prayer to alleviate shame

Body, first capital & I have bartered it
oh God, oh trined mother, I have
spent it story awash in the stench
of what feeds me I am not
what I have done to get here
Body, trusted compass, somehow
we have always made it out alive
& isn't that what this miraculous
shroud was fashioned for   this dazzling machine
allow me to test the limits of what the senses
can take I am starting to unravel my obsession
with what carries us upright & tangled

a bullet sails past the third moon
& I claw rivers into my
                                        Body, unholiest of muses

each breath that escapes is its own penance.

Irene & I forget to take our birth control   again

being the granddaughter of a colony means I am a real giver   sometimes, mid give
I remember the feeling of being owned by what you never asked for & an empire's worth of
history pours out my unhinged jaw

                 [medical researchers take the pill trials to Puerto Rico to prove
                     even poor, uneducated women could use it successfully]

       I am not successful at anything but tidying my legs to be opened

my grandmother's cigarettes are martyring prayers in their little glass chapel
plastic beads lacing through the dunes of charred bodies

which reminds me that I need to start lighting candles   again
light as many as it takes until God answers   again

       because it is the second week of the month   again

& my underwear are as clean as a clinic   again

dermatillomania aka **how my anxiety shows up** aka **what my mother passed down to me**

I chase light each day

                                     more so flame

seduced by that which occupies

                   & consumes

I spend too many minutes weighing the future   its ghosts

which saint do I pray to when the need to feast

              on fleeting moments

becomes the devouring of skin

                    I hope to reincarnate as something

                    that does not have teeth

conversation with Irene through the curtain in the aftercare room

after Safia Elhillo

I told myself the first one was the last one

they gave me the orange juice

which is more like orange drink but I can't keep anything down because I can't keep anything

no, I don't regret it

it wasn't forced on me this time but I'm not sure I'm meant to be a mother

        yet   you've had fifteen? does that make you like the god of abortions?

my apologies

that was a bad joke

does it ever get better ?

being in charge of a body & all of its madness

is that what a mother is supposed to teach you?

my mother never taught me how to swim, you know

can't even tread water herself

I almost drowned once at a birthday party

everyone else knew how to swim

in your book, you talk about all the sailing you've done

I wonder what that would be like but along with the inability to swim

I also have motion sickness

&

a body that feels like an already sunken ship

airless   &   haunted

Lolita sells her body to pay the rent

& she knows that everything can be used
the body :   first currency   :   most mined resource

I want a god that does what She must to survive
Mary Magdalene perched on scabbed knees
praying to the moon & a book's worth of bad women

I have never had to trade my remains for cover or coin
though I know of bartering pieces & parts to keep the pit of me
filled   or   warmed   or   remembered

Lolita spends twenty-seven years in prison
for attempting to overthrow Amerik³a's rule
tired of the mining & by mining
I mean raping
what is home but a place that gets taken

              & taken

                & taken

          & t a
                k   e

                n

what is the body but a foul coin sleeping at the bottom of a pseudo silk sea

awaiting the rubbed pleasure of a transactional finger

aguacate

take the womb

cut around the pit

as is done with its distant

sister - the avocado

spoon it out of skin

add salt & lemon to keep

spread it on seeded toast

charge contempo colonizers

nine dollars for slathered insides

& when they complain

about a belly full of ghosts

open your legs as wide

as interpretation

      & show them the empty trees

speaking to the miscarried about their choice of setting

in the days before the living   there was you

who arrived on that evening as I plotted my inevitable exodus

from a part-time job at the jewelry store in the mall

you would've been a difficult babything

because of the dramatics in your arrival & immediate departure

couldn't wait until I clocked out at least made it home to clean towels & already stained carpet

no   you had to cascade out all startling   & red   as in   we cannot go any further

                                        [the princess cuts blushed with embarrassment

                        the diamond tennis bracelets complained about the cherry distraction

                        & the gold recognized the smell of what it belongs to]

why did you have to make such a mess of us

                                        rudely smearing yourself across the white leather stool

listen   I am sorry to place blame like this

clearly my body has a hard time accepting its failures   its inability to finish what it starts

there isn't much to say really except   I will always remember your brief hour

the halogen lights that caught the luster of your best angles

 the unspooling of ruby after ruby

                &rubies&rubies&rubies

at the hospital, I will learn your blood was not my type & so

I pray to my troubled god
to soften your passage, Intruder
Precious Gem

3 women [dead] from pill trials

sugar mapping

Amerik³a says I smell sweet & that the stench of me lingers. says it makes their mouth water.
I am a delicacy. an ache on the tongue. when Amerik³a touches me I turn into sugar water. in my
head Celia Cruz shouts *Azucar!* as each wave promises to ease a stuck hunger.

my grandmother loved Celia & shouting in praise of the shared export of their cousin islands.
joyful worship in debt to sugar. dysplastic cells dance in the second neck of her. my grandmother.
stuck on sugar. carried egg & trait & passed them down. like a recipe. a curse. Celia's head is
slicked with a sweetness for which there is no cure. & so no one shouts *Azucar!* out loud anymore.

sugarcane harvesting is one of the hardest forms of labor there is, besides giving birth. Lolita
birthed a sugarcane baby. what does that make her labor? Gladys, the sugarcane baby, receives
a hysterectomy after bearing too many children for Amerik³a's taste. hysteria has the same root
word as hysterectomy & I know both mean it is unlucky to be uterus-ed. hysteria is the devil in
the milk.

sugar causes the body to eat itself. away. I am a salt water taffy oroborus. the kind of sucrose
serpent that threatens to colonize the teeth. black holes preluding decay. I tell Amerik³a I am
more than the history of my cavities. Amerik³a laughs as it turns the last of my crystaled parts
into a cloying chaos.

delicacy

I did not mean to paint us willing
that is just how it sounds in english
let us be something other than colonizer porn
spicy mamis, hot guinea pigs
                              pigs feet taste like a stewed freeing
give us soiled parts & we will make a feast
survival means no part unused

my mother's legs are a topography
of indigo rivers a new one appears
at the mouth of her body each time
she remembers that squealing taste
& the feeling of the citrine sun on her
skin I want to become something
other than what has been done to me

I once kissed a boy who thanked me for my history
& by kissed I mean fucked
& by thank I mean apologized
said he was sorry for being a trigger
the same rind as pigs feet
I tell him my only form of birth control is the moon
& a god I made up
I was taught bodies are as effective as weapons

& still
no ones knows what happened back then
but my god & all Her ghosts
I tried to listen for their calls but

                              couldn't hear a thing over all the squealing

blood mapping

FADE IN:

AMERIK³A'S EXAM ROOM - DAY
(Little Body, Amerik³a)

WE OPEN ON LITTLE BODY, 29 YEARS INHABITED. BODY LIES ON THE EXAM
TABLE NAKED FROM THE WAIST DOWN. LITTLE BODY IS HERE FOR AN IUD
REMOVAL. AMERIK³A ENTERS HASTILY.

AMERIK³A

What form of control will you now be taking in the IUDs absence?

LITTLE BODY

I was planning on halting all forms of control.

AMERIK³A

I don't feel comfortable not having some form of control over you. Believe
me, I know how feverishly you can produce.

LITTLE BODY
(to the camera)

The truth is I learned of Amerik³a's fetish with territory & the wombs that create it
Which caused me to develop a fetish for decolonizing the only land I can claim
I wet at the idea of leaving chance to the moon & a makebelieve god

LITTLE BODY
(to Amerik³a)

I am to be someone's wedded property soon & want to fulfill a planned pregnancy.

AMERIK³A

(SNORTS) There is a first time for everything.

AMERIK³A READIES SWELLED FINGERS. THE LAUGH TRACK CUTS IN. LITTLE
BODY'S SLICK SHAME UNCLAPS ITS SCARRED KNEES AND LOOKS THE
OTHER WAY.

the 3 R's of Amerik³an medical experimentation, 1956

Rabbits

Rats

Ricans

k³ [kuotes from the kolonizing kind]

It is better for all the world, if instead of waiting to execute degenerate offspring for crime, or to let them starve for imbecility, society can prevent those who are manifestly unfit from continuing their kind

I have studied with interest the laws of several American states concerning prevention of reproduction by people whose progeny would, in all probability, be of no value or be injurious to the racial stock

Your army of occupation

More children for the fit, less for the unfit

Reckless breeders

..the gradual suppression, elimination and eventual extinction, of defective stocks — those human weeds which threaten the blooming of the finest flowers of American civilization

Given Birth Control   *the unfit will voluntarily eliminate their kind*

Birth Control does not mean contraception indiscriminately practised, it means the release and cultivation of the better elements in our society

Birth Control must lead ultimately to   *a cleaner race*

The availability of the operation is quite apparent, and for women who cannot afford the cost-and most public hospitals charge only twenty-five to thirty dollars-

a blood donation of two pints is accepted in payment

...the Porto Ricans — they are beyond doubt the dirtiest, laziest, most degenerate and thievish race of men to ever inhabit this sphere

What the island needs is not public health work, but a tidal wave or something to totally exterminate the entire population, it might then

be livable

[monologue with dance: the angel of redemption]

FADE IN:

COUNCIL TABLE IN HEAVEN
(God, Self)

SELF IS AUDITIONING FOR THE PART OF "THE ANGEL OF REDEMPTION."
SELF SITS ACROSS FROM GOD. ONE FOOT ON THE SEAT OF THE CHAIR, THE
OTHER SWINGING, BARELY TOUCHING THE GROUND. SELF SPEAKS SELLING-
LY THROUGH A HALO OF SMOKE.

SELF

I have a gift for charming myself into the soft places
quite the collection of brilliantly malleable bones
willing to open like a sky for just the right pitch
sometimes, if I part my mouth just enough
I can taste what I cannot afford to buy back
breathe in radiant ash   first sugaring of the story

                              I have a gift for holding tight to history
                it always comes back to the past, because the future is a void
                      is an obsession - ask the skin on Little Body's hands
                someone has to pay back the dirt with what it craves most
                           I can at least offer a word or three
                    perhaps the body   first currency of the divine

SELF LIGHTS A CIGARETTE. FRUITLESS SHADOWS BEGIN TO RISE. PERFORM A RITUAL DANCE FOR GOD. BELLS FORGED OF COPPER AND LIGHTNING TWINE SCABBED ANKLES. CLINKING A BATTLE SONG AS TENSE AS THE HUSK THAT AWAITS FIRSTBITE.

                                    SELF
                                 (EXHALES)
                    I assure you - a tithing soon come.

sonnet in pill form

It is a Wednesday like any & there is overpriced coffee &

women of the colonizing kind modeling perfectly practiced sad faces

without anything to really be sad about. What I'm saying

is my ancestors are disappointed. There

is a button to my left that's yelling *my body, my business*

& now I am as steaming as the almond-oat-dandelion house

mylk. I want the button to choke on its privilege. Its

seven dollar latte. Like the women on the island that is

much too owned to consider choked on tiny pill bombs &

the smoke coming from cauterized parts. What I'm saying

is someone too poor & too fertile & too erased gave

the body donning the button its right to business & choice.

The steam simmers to a plant based sorrow when I think

of how everything that pledges freedom comes with a body count.

sailor, oh, sailor

mira, whatever you do, don't stand inside of it, my mother warns me

it is a particular corner of the Bermuda triangle that lives in one of the outposts at El Morro

one of your cousins did & you know what happened to him?

he was struck by lightning

My womb is the Bermuda triangle   what makes it in, does not come out

I do not say this to my mother   would rather share ghost stories

With strangers on this sinking ship   I know my audience &

We all have secrets too heavy to float   Anyway, back to the confession no one asked for

You see, I am exaggerating again   as all good tour guides do

There were two ships that passed &   made it safe to shore

I want to stop using metaphors for the things no one wishes to hear

I had my first abortion at 17   & I don't regret it

The next at 19   & I don't regret it

shame is a moonless night

that offers no absolution   so I have extracted it too

& instead light a candle for Irene, Patron Saint of Impossible Mothers

pray to the three headed god She belongs to   *[please aspirate each "unlawful sin"]*

national anthem in the key of Lolita

all lines pulled from "La Borinqueña" by Lola Rodriguez de Tío

Land of

Borinquén, daughter of sea & sun   *It is time to fight!*

The machete will speak *victory or death*

Borinquén must be machete sharpened

Be free machete sharpened nation

Unconquerable women

Freedom awaits

Anxiously

Freedom

Freedom.

my womb is a dance
of leaves sweating swift winds
i laugh with guitars

SONIA SANCHEZ

new god flow (a Kanye West & Pusha T erasure)

I believe I'm the God of holes

                      write it in spirit

                                  good killer I came for more

gold

      more

      shake that rare body

                     come and have a good time with a new god

breathe stars   sell

            Death by threes

see my luxury

         sold in want

a Crown   a brick

when you flood you drown, golden child

hold me down, Body

         most hated god

three dreams

no resolution

      til we drown   in peace

sold people

made from mess

               the world

                                      3 dreams

like there God go

barely

mama   [Lolita]   ran up   shot

mom   [Gladys]   in the street

[Irene]   follow the water   the cane

make the new fire

annihilate body

violate body

I've been told

I'm

Some   Body

Genesis 3:16

Unto the woman he said

I will greatly multiply thy sorrow and thy conception;

 in sorrow thou shalt bring forth children;

 and thy desire shall be to thy husband,

 and he shall rule over thee.

Ginese 3:16

Unto the mothers I say

We will greatly multiply our legacy & our stories;

      in joy we shall bring forth children;

       & our desire shall be for ourselves,

        & fuck what you heard...

Lolita writes an op-ed on parenting

Beyond myself, I am something other than a mother
Beyond this shoreline, I am something other than occupied

Until I reach the next shoreline, then I am a cipher
Oh, what we could be full of if anyone knew
The right way to hold a gun in the atomic age

As in   I am trying to make the world a better place for the future
As in   the child is wise enough to know that this is bigger than them
As in   what does it matter if only one of us survives

We are nothing without the people who hold us   together

As in   if I have taught you nothing, child
Let me at least teach you how to think beyond your self

If I don't see my self as a nation, how will I know where the bombs end & I begin

If I don't see my self as a mother, but more so a movement
How will I know the differing pitch of a battle cry from a hunger cry

Don't both deserve a warm sip of salted milk from the teta of a country that claims to know
their ache

What good are children if they are made of mere sacrifice

I will not wreck my body to birth anything other than a revolution.

Puerto Rico, January 2020

it is the 47th anniversary of Roe v. Wade
& I am in Puerto Rico

a dig through the womb of this commonly unwealthy
commonwealth will note the significance of me awakening

to a sickness that vibrates communal
On this day meant to service disruption

I eat a moon of mallorca
chase it with café con leche

A familiar communion to banish this possession
out of my body   my head hurricanes

a dizziness that cannot be mine alone
skin dewed with the water of work

I am a powerless satellite
unlit by even the most tenacious of suns

                                   [history - hysteria :
                                            an embittered woman's heirloom]

in this case of generational symptoms bloodied
deep in the layers of this sugarsored island of trial & error

After error after error after
//: err___//: or

                // how long does it take for the effects of colonialism to subside?

leech

In this water I am a jewel fastened
to the infinite darkness of bottom dwelling
Both my mouths eat of wonder &
gore I pray to the god of the pull out
that my sins stay unnamed /
my b o d y stays bloodletting & tender
as a worm Sometimes I am as ready as
I am willing Other times the story smells
of soured wood & I forget that I am
not always alone that there is company I take
a cigarette from the freezer
Pour lost blood from one cup into another
temperant yet drunk off my own wine
I smile with all my cherried teeth

hysteria in the lunar age aka **the body poetic**

<u>FADE IN:</u>

<u>CEIBA TREE BY THE RIVER - NIGHT</u>
(Little Body, Gladys)

LITTLE BODY AND GLADYS SIT UNDER A CEIBA TREE BY THE RIVER. THEY
PASS A CIGARETTE BACK AND FORTH. BOTH LOOK IN OPPOSITE DIRECTIONS
TOWARDS SOMETHING THAT ISN'T THERE.

LITTLE BODY

I can say I am a poet because I have written words in my own clot & I am as tragic as I
am flexible. & yes, I get turned on by the moon. Like any obedient poet. & I would, you
know...fuck the moon. & yes, I realize I've assigned the moon to be my god but honestly,
who doesn't want a god they can

GLADYS

Forget when the time comes. Forget the touch of what is asking you to stay. Forget the
hands you leave behind. Sometimes you make choices. Sometimes choices make you.

LITTLE BODY

Why do I always hunger for what adds the most viscosity to the poem? I bend open &
words rejoice. Pulpy stories tumble out of my warmest mouth. & then there is the moon
again because what a poet births must be witnessed by their obsession

& how many times do I have to call myself something before it becomes a

law

known   history

curse

GLADYS

Sometimes you don't understand that the history is its own curse. Not until it's too late.
Not until they've taken everything. All of your moons. & you let them because what

58

choice do you really have. Choice is an illusion. Because the options are presented to you. Not chosen by you.

GLADYS PASSES THE CIGARETTE BACK FOR THE LAST TIME AND LOOKS AT LITTLE BODY FOR THE FIRST TIME.

Choice is a privilege. What will you do with yours?

LITTLE BODY

I choose to become the poem   ink the story in all of this escaped blood
            test how well my wounds perform in a clinical trial of the night sky

de·col·o·ni·za·tion

noun

/ I sever myself from Amerik³a / cleave the taxed cord / contaminate the water with gold & sugar / somehow / I float on

use over time for: decolonization

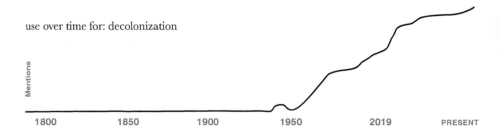

Mentions

1800   1850   1900   1950   2019   PRESENT

a puta's requiem

night: a velveteen pandemonium

all the stars sing a lament about having survived a grim deal

solely running off sugar & smoke

so smoke

I must then   a fiftyfourth studio head spin

eyes ziplip   I hemorrhage myself into a seat

the moons scheme hysteric above

                    &

I am held by the idea of a forgiving god

as I inhale my deepest shadows

nauseous spirits orbit back to their abandoned bodies

mothers&daughters&babies

allthebabies
&&&

at the top of the cosmic table squats God, The Forgiving
three headed & gestating with rebellion

babies & the phantoms of them pudding out
like globs of sweet rice

from halogen bowls strewn across the table
all the mothers & almost mothers howl

silicone cups full of omnipotent sangria
overflow with the romance of dark curses

      [s i l e n c e]

God tucks Herself into a curl of respect for herself
the rest of us follow suit

draw a circle with our sharpest nail atop swollen lips
vow to become something other than the choices we've made

                                        I want more
                                         children
                                         because
                                           they
                                           told
                                            me
                                           not
                                            to

        I want fertile land to sow and a wiped debt and
          strong coffee without blood in the grounds
              I want no more blood on the ground
             I want a ground that is soft with growth
                   I don't want to own it
                    I just want to tend it
                  This land, I don't own
                  My children, I don't own
            Ownership kills the spirit of a thing

I want more
freedom
because
they
told
me
not
to

I am succumbing to the truth, but this time I move beyond just surviving it

As heads rise
bellies gorge
we are
pregnant
with
unvoy
aged
oce
an
s

& secret gold

I am tasked with placing a coin on the eye of a dim child
as cold metal touches cold skin
the mothers&daughters&babies
become a plume of spirit

I pick the skin off my occupied hands
because I am always trying to get to the meat
of the story
the hot pain of skin leaving hands beckons the raising of eyelids
I welcome the milk of light into my most active hole

& finally, something lives long enough to tell the tale

& finally, in my own name

I pray.

I've been nobody's child
I've been nobody's child
So my blood started running wild
Oh my blood started running wild
I've been a lonely girl
I've been a lonely girl
But I'm ready for the world
Oh I'm ready for the world
Well I'm ready for the world

HURRAY FOR THE RIFF RAFF

second birth

newly emerged from the motherwound of God, Little Body carries
Self through a threshold of barbed edges

Little Body does not ask for much besides a warm bed
& some puff   small thing, precious & forgiving, is most Self-less

at night   opening for anything that might stay long enough to see
Little Body can do tricks   turn slither & beast with a flash of

bonetooth when it meets the flesh just so   what filth Little Body is
capable of   [replace *filth* with *healing*, for here they mean the same]

Self does not ask for much besides the freedom to talk of the dark
& some respect on her name   Self was made into a little fire

by creatorspirits who say bitch! with their fangs & spend
their vacant hours smoking cigarettes held by claws red as warning

[Self & Little Body meld together, create I -
as in *I am as resilient as a crucifix*]

I have never belonged to anything but the moon or the ghosts
of my sisters   who are not really my sisters but what I mean

is understood   I want to smoke cigarettes religiously
as in I am willing to tar my throat for the sake of worship

though, I don't like going to the doctor or I don't have health
insurance   both are true so my rowdiest hole stays supple

& unfixed   anyway, back to the story about what I owe my life to
really, it's all of this   a council of girlmothers who answer prayers

69

faster than any mangod the foolish can claim   however,
do not be misled   it isn't always this way   they do not wake everyday
tied to their survival   sometimes when the problems are away
the council sighs   each of them lighting a harmless cigarette

kicking their well walked shoes off   a bloodbirth of their favorite songs
melting from the window

the whole time laughing like dogs.

NOTES

Information & details gathered from the books *Impossible Motherhood: Testimony of an Abortion Addict* & *The Ladies' Gallery: A Memoir of Family Secrets* by Irene Vilar, as well as the documentary *La Operación* by Ana María García

"conversation with Irene through the curtain in the aftercare room" is after the poem "late-night phone call with abdelhalim hafez" by Safia Elhillo

"undertow" is titled after the song "Undertow" by Warpaint

"k3 [kuotes from the kolonizing kind]" is quoted from multiple eugenics enthusiasts that have held high esteem in the American medical world, their names aren't worth mentioning

"national anthem in the key of Lolita" borrows all lines from "La Borinqueña" by Lola Rodriguez de Tio

"new god flow (a Kanye West & Pusha T erasure)" borrows all lines from "New God Flow" by Kanye West & Pusha T

"genesis / ginese" borrows lines from the Bible verse, Genesis 3:16

SHOUTOUTS

Thank you to the editors of these journals who first published previous versions of these poems:

"la operación aka when he asks if I'm on birth control" - first version in *Chifladazine*, second version in *Palabritas*

"undertow" in *Homology Lit*

"sonnet in pill form" & "delicacy" in *Wax Nine Journal*

"that time I made a joke about all the girls in our history class being part of the plan b team" & "hijadelagranputa" in *Moko Magazine*

•

First & foremost, the most sacred of shoutouts to God, whatever that may mean & wherever it may exist.

To Giovanni & Rocco, all of my belief & faith in anything good lies within the both of you. Words could never do enough to express the depths of my love for you. Thank you for the infinite amount of patience, understanding, & support you allowed me during this process. Being a published author is pretty sick, but being your mother is the absolute sickest.

To Mom, for life, my love of reading, really stellar genes, & the charisma to bring it all home. Thank you for every single thing. Dad, for aiding in the providing of said life & stellar genes but also for the gift of good humor. I love you both tremendously. To my Cordero family, thank you for the history, the culture, & the immense love. I owe what I am to our shared blood. My Ginese family, thank you for all the grace & love. Sam,

Candace, Daad, & Teta, your love, care, & time dedicated to Gio & Rocco allowed me the space to write. I am tremendously grateful to count y'all as family. To Margie & Dominic, from being my down-the-street-parents to my children's godparents, you've been by my side during life's biggest moments & you were never obligated to which means something special. I love you so very much. To the Gonzalez, Candelario, Santiago, & Torres-Hall families - thank you for inviting me into your homes & for always allowing me to overstay my welcome.

THIS BOOK WOULD NOT HAVE BEEN POSSIBLE WITHOUT THE HOLIEST OF HOLY DAYS KNOWN AS "STRUGGLE SUNDAY." To Ali, my honest-to-God life partner, I can't say thank you enough. May our treats never unsweeten & our summers be forever endless. Ilyia, your support through everything has been monumental. We shooting a movie this summer at K Kream. There will be dead presidents & crunch coat as far as the eye can see. Britt, you've been such a source of encouragement the entire way through. Thank you for pulling me out of countless early morning anxiety swirls, although I'm certain we ain't seen the last of them. I love y'all more than I know how to articulate, mis perras mejores.

Baleigh - My Ace - My Fool, we one stop closer to our baller dreams. I can't wait to cut up in Mykonos or some shit with you. Thank you for being a forever rider, I love you.

To TJ, for the deed on the title & recognizing when a bar is a bar. I'm ridiculously appreciative of you & your existence in general. Thank you for being here. Thank you for letting me in. Everyone who is not already hip, go type "Peachcurls" into your streaming apps & run the songs all the way UP…Escalades await!

Lynette & Catherine, the red string of this book was found through my collaboration & experiences with y'all. That's pretty sick. I love you both like family, thank you.

To the crew, the gang, the fam: Ramon, thanks for always giving me a space to share my shit, for checking in, & suggesting the most fire food spots. You're a real one. Los & Maneet, for being the sweetest sweeties & providing me endless dancefloors to cut up on. You've shown me how deep the love of family goes. I love y'all. Zoë, my G-est of G's, for all the love & hype. Let's get this diamond encrusted bag. Kyle, thanks for being a solid homie & faithful reader. The cover literally would not have come together without you, so a big shoutout to you. Sarah, my South Lorain Italian Stallion, thank you for your fire ass support & yoga instruction. Bernie, Elie, Diana, Nate, & Kaisito -

thank you for keeping me full of wine & snacks & for supporting my work just cause it came from me. Y'all are a gift. Titi loves you, Kaisito! To the realest of ones, Mia, I've never even met you in person but you've been supporting & sharing my writing since jump. It has meant the world. I wish you nothing but peace, abundance, & the fattest of blunts.

The loudest of shoutouts to Kevin, Brendan, & the rest of Grieveland for giving this wayward book a home. To Kevin especially, a shoutout for consistently supporting my work & always extending opportunities to me. Also, for being the raddest birthday twin around.

To the Julia de Burgos Cultural Arts Center, whose support through the Unidos Por El Arte grant provided the funds that allowed me to finish this collection on a new Macbook.

To Carolina, thank you for bringing your style to my words. Your intention & thoughtfulness really made the cover everything it is…a Bori-punk dream!

To Kisha, "thank you" isn't a sufficient enough expression to convey the gratitude, love, & respect I have for you. I can honestly say my life as a writer would not be what it is if it weren't for you. You & Love are so loved. Noor, deep gratitude for the love & feedback on this work. Your words of encouragement kept this book afloat. Isabella, for your incredible support & friendship. Quartez, YOOO…for the phone calls, the good news, & your impeccable homie-ship. Eric, for all the hype, laughs, & smoke sessions provided. Naaz, for all the talks & deeply spirited hugs. To Raja, Mary, Ephraim, Daniel, Matt, Michelle, Jason, Sarah, Krysia, Jing, & the rest of the Cleveland literary community, thank you for the support & kind words each time our paths crossed & for the countless opportunities y'all have provided. To Cierra, Leila, Tizziana, & the rest of the SPACES crew, thanks for supporting in monumental ways individually & as a team. I wholeheartedly enjoy spending my weekdays with y'all. A colossal thank you to all the homies that reside within the city of Cleveland & beyond, thank you for every share, re-post, & order. The love is felt & it is returned tenfold.

To the memory of Chispa, my favorite storyteller & first best friend…

& the memories of Emma, Paca, Jordan, Mary, & Iris - the most supreme heavenly council

& finally, to you - dear reader, wherever you are & whomever you may be, know that I am eternally grateful to you for allowing my words to take up space in your head. I wish you all the goodness in this life & the ones that lie beyond.

Thank you.

STEPHANIE GINESE is a writer & wannabe comedian from South Lorain, Ohio. She is the daughter of a Puerto Rican mother & an Italian immigrant father. She currently lives in Cleveland, by the lake, with her two children. This is her debut book of poetry.

CPSIA information can be obtained
at www.ICGtesting.com
Printed in the USA
JSHW012104010623
42551JS00006B/404